CLASSICAL**PIECES**FOR
SOLOGUITAR

18 Classical Masterpieces Arranged for the Advancing Guitarist

ROB**THORPE**

FUNDAMENTAL**CHANGES**

Classical Pieces for Solo Guitar

18 Classical Masterpieces Arranged for the Advancing Guitarist

Published by **www.fundamental-changes.com**

ISBN: 978-1-78933-219-3

Copyright © 2020 Rob Thorpe

www.fundamental-changes.com

Over 11,000 fans on Facebook: **FundamentalChangesInGuitar**

Instagram: **FundamentalChanges**

For over 350 Free Guitar Lessons with Videos Check Out

www.fundamental-changes.com

Cover Image Copyright: Shutterstock, Tommaso Lizzul

Contents

Foreword   5

Practice and Performance Tips   6

Get the Audio   7

1. Irish Medley   8

2. Study No.1, Op. 31, Fernando Sor   12

3. In the Bleak Midwinter – Gustav Holst   16

4. Waltz in C Major, Op. 27 – Ferdinando Carulli   20

5. Greensleeves – Traditional   24

6. Minuet in G Major – attr. J.S. Bach   28

7. The Four Seasons – Antonio Vivaldi   33

8. Symphony No.9, Mvt. 4 "Ode to Joy" – Ludwig Van Beethoven   38

9. Ride of the Valkyries – Richard Wagner   43

10. In the Hall of the Mountain King – Edvard Grieg   50

11. Symphony No.40 – W.A. Mozart   55

12. Study No.9, Op. 35 – Fernando Sor   61

13. Für Elise – Ludwig van Beethoven   67

14. Theme from the 24th Caprice – Niccolo Paganini   72

15. Slavonic Dance No.1 – Antonín Dvořák   75

16. Hornpipe – George Frederick Handel   81

17. Pictures at an Exhibition (Promenade) – Modest Mussorgsky   86

18. Great Gate of Kiev – Modest Mussorgsky   90

Closing Words   94

By the Same Author   95

Contents

Foreword

Welcome to my book which focuses on introducing famous classical music into your repertoire. The aim is to get you up and running quickly, playing the music of great classical composers. These pieces include many famous melodies, most of which you'll recognise.

A few of the included pieces were originally composed for the guitar by Fernando Sor and Ferdinando Carulli, while other pieces are from famous orchestral works by Beethoven, Mozart and Vivaldi, which I have arranged for solo guitar. However, what links all the pieces are strong, recognisable melodies.

At first sight, classical guitar can seem difficult and teaching methods often prescribe many repetitive technical exercises and scales. While these can be beneficial, they shouldn't overshadow the main goal of having fun making music, which is why I've created a library of pieces that are both fun and satisfying, while remaining accessible to beginner guitarists.

Learning to read traditional music notation has many benefits, but I feel strongly that students who want to play guitar for their own pleasure should be able to do so immediately. That's why every piece is written here in standard notation and tablature.

I hope you find these pieces fun and rewarding, and that they help you grow as a musician.

But above all, have fun!

Enjoy the journey!

Rob

Practice and Performance Tips

Regular practice is crucial to making progress on any musical instrument, and developing good practice habits will pay dividends in accelerating your proficiency. Committing to short, regular practice is the best approach. Give time to focus on specific trouble spots, as well as enjoying playing longer sections of a piece.

Each of the eighteen pieces in this book is accompanied by extensive notes which include technical advice regarding trouble spots you might encounter and exercises to help you overcome them. However, broader technical instruction is beyond the scope of this book, so I suggest you use this repertoire volume in conjunction with a more general method book, such as the *Classical Guitar Technique Book* by Diego Prato, or lessons with a local guitar tutor.

At all times it's important to play with musicality and an even tempo. Listen to my performances in the audio examples to help you internalise any tricky rhythms. Find a comfortable speed where the notes can be played with control and good tone. Your progress will be quicker by practicing slowly but with good tone, rather than racing to play quickly and sloppily.

Throughout the book I will suggest picking and fingering patterns. Picking-hand digits use the following letters: *P* (thumb) *I* (index) *M* (middle) *A* (ring) in the accompanying text. Fretting-hand fingerings will be marked above the notation by numbers 1-4, going from the index finger to pinky.

I will occasionally refer to playing in numerical positions on the fretboard. This indicates where the first finger is resting, even if we're playing using other digits. For example, playing in "fourth position" means the first finger is resting on the fourth fret.

To achieve the traditional classical tone there's no real substitute for letting your picking-hand fingernails grow. Unfortunately, long nails don't coexist well with daily life and filing them carefully to get the best connection to the string becomes a regular commitment. There are a range of synthetic fake nails available that are popular with steel-string acoustic players, but you can simply use the flesh of your fingertips to settle for a warmer, quieter tone.

While playing this music on a nylon-string classical guitar will provide the most authentic sound, any acoustic guitar will do equally well to get you started.

Get the Audio

The audio files for this book are available to download for *free* from **www.fundamental-changes.com.** The link is available via the top line of the **fundamental-changes** home page. Simply select "Guitar" then this book title from the drop-down menu and follow the instructions to get the audio.

We recommend that you download these files directly to your computer (not to your tablet) and extract them from there before adding them to your media library. Having done so you can transfer them on your tablet, iPod, or burn them to CD. On the download page there's a 'Help' PDF and *we also provide technical support via the form on the download page.*

We put a lot of care into getting these audios just right and you'll greatly benefit by listening to the examples as you work through the book. They're free, so what are you waiting for?!

Head over to **www.fundamental-changes.com** and grab the audio files now.

There are also over 350 free guitar lessons to get your teeth into.

1. Irish Medley

Sally Gardens - Drowsy Maggie - Dick Gossip's Reel

To kick off this collection of beginner pieces we have a medley of popular tunes from Ireland's rich heritage of folk music. It's common for several similar tunes to be linked together into a longer piece, often intended for people to dance to. Our medley begins with a tune known as an *air*, before picking up the pace with two *reels*.

Airs are slow melodic pieces that aren't really intended for dance. The main dances are *jigs, reels, polkas* and *hornpipes*, each of which has a unique character and pulse.

In this piece, the melody is unaccompanied, which will let you focus on linking the notes on the neck, achieving a good tone, and learning to move from string to string comfortably with both hands.

Sally Gardens is a poem, written by the Irish poet W.B. Yeats, which was later set to music by Herbert Hughes using a traditional tune called *Maids of Mourne Shore*. The word "Sally" refers to the willow tree (*salix*), from the Gaelic "saileach".

An air like *Sally Gardens* provides a gentle, atmospheric opening to the piece. The phrasing should be relaxed and rhythmically free flowing. Learning the words and keeping them in mind will help you to give the music more expression.

All three pieces in this medley use the D Major scale, so familiarising yourself with the notes will speed up your progress when playing the ascending and descending melodies. Even though we rarely play scales within pieces of music, musicians practice them to train their fingers and ears to recognise common sequences and patterns.

Consistency is key, so make sure you follow the fretting hand fingerings above the notation.

Example 1a

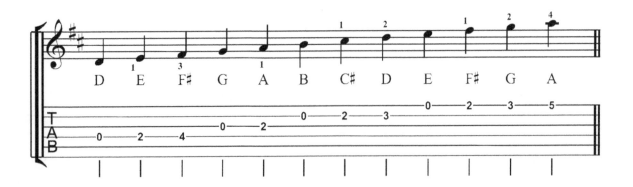

Why not use the notes to write a folk tune of your own? Doing this will help to reinforce the sound of the scale, and the intervals between the different notes within it.

The second tune is *Drowsy Maggie*. This reel dates back to the mid-19th century, but is now widely recognised from the film *Titanic*, during the ceilidh (pronounced *kay-lee*) dance scene. The tempo is much faster than *Sally Gardens* and is played with an even pulse. You'll need to practise it thoroughly, so there are no pauses or hesitation when you play. Thankfully, there are several repeating patterns, so it's not as daunting as it may seem.

The tune has two eight-bar sections; the first is bars 15-18 (played twice) and the second is bars 20-27.

Learning to play the two important bars below in advance will help you tackle the rest of the piece. Pay attention to the picking pattern using *P* (thumb) and *I* (index). Practise each one until you can repeat it on a loop without dropping the pulse.

Example 1b

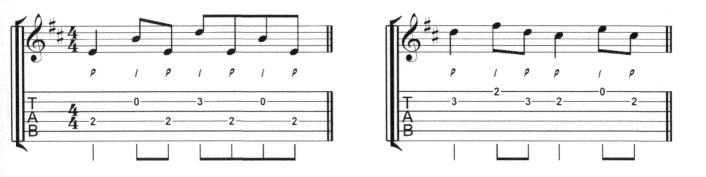

The third tune is *Dick Gossip's Reel*. This tune makes heavy use of the high E string with only occasional notes on the B and G strings. The best approach is to pluck with alternating index and middle fingers (*I* and *M*) while resting the thumb on an unused low string.

There's more repetition here and the first six bars end with the same descending four notes. So, while the two full pages may look daunting, there's not nearly as much material to learn as you might think.

In bar thirty-five, the note F (1st fret, high E string) should be played with the first finger. To accommodate this, the preceding notes at the 3rd fret are played with the third finger. The first finger can then move back up to the 2nd fret as you return to bar twenty-eight as shown below.

Example 1c

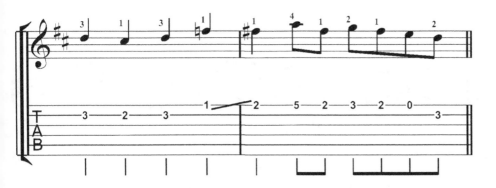

Irish Folk Medley

Dick Gossip's Reel

2. Study No.1, Op. 31, Fernando Sor

Fernando Sor is probably the most important composer in the history of classical guitar. He produced a great number of pieces, ranging from beginner etudes such as this one, right through to demanding concert repertoire. His pieces have remained popular with students and teachers, both for their musical appeal and their effectiveness in developing technical ability.

Sor's impact as a composer, performer and teacher brought the guitar to a new level of respectability, where previously it had been seen as a "lower" folk instrument, compared to other orchestral instruments.

Sor was born in 1778 in Barcelona and was educated as a chorister at the Montserrat monastery in Catalonia before moving to Madrid, aged twenty. He was sympathetic to the regime in Spain installed by Napoleon Bonaparte, so when it fell he was exiled. He settled in Paris, but also spent time in London and Moscow. While celebrated in his day, he was largely forgotten after his death in 1839, until a revival of his work was championed by Andrés Segovia.

This study is from Op. 31, a collection of twenty-four short *études*. Études are short pieces of music written to be both educational and musical. This piece includes instances of playing two simultaneous notes that should be performed with the picking thumb and finger in a pinching motion.

I've notated best fingerings wherever it might otherwise be unclear. One example is in bars 7-8 shown below. Many students find the combination of fingers 2 and 4 awkward at first, but developing this skill now will pay off in future.

Example 2a

Again, isolating difficult passages is the most effective practice approach.

In bars 23-25 several two-finger note pairs are played in quick succession that require different combinations of fingers to be used, which can present a challenge to both your independence and coordination. Practise each pair of notes separately, then link one pair to the next slowly to make sure you stay relaxed.

The following short study will help you to work on this. Open-string notes are placed between each two-note chord to give you more time to change. Eventually, you should be able to hold one shape right until the moment you move to the next shape, but to begin with, your only focus should be on putting your fingers down at the same time as you pluck.

Example 2b

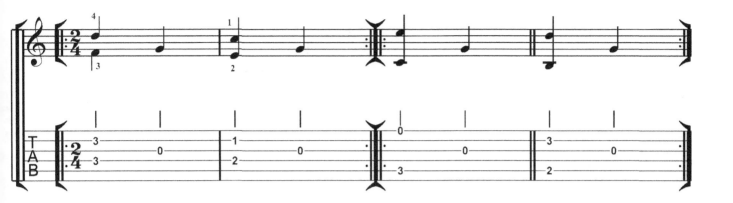

You'll see that the tails of some notes face upwards, and others downwards. The former are the tune and the latter are bass notes. Bass notes provide a rhythmic foundation and imply chord changes. This gives your performance a more three-dimensional feel. To understand how bass and melody notes work together, here is a study based on bars fifteen and sixteen.

The lower note should be held throughout, while the higher notes alternate. Focus on anchoring one fretting hand finger to the fretboard while the other finger moves on and off.

Example 2c

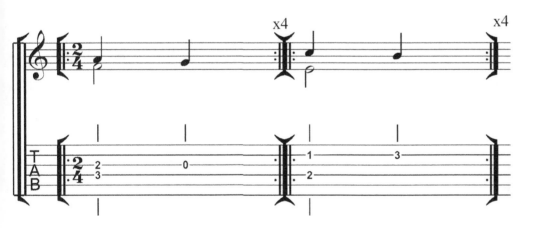

Once you can play the exercise, listen to each of the parts. Shift your attention from the long low note to the alternating high notes to train your ears to hear the different layers within the music.

Study No.1, Op. 31 – Fernando Sor

3. In the Bleak Midwinter – Gustav Holst

Gustav Holst is one of England's most famous composers. His best-known work is the orchestral suite *The Planets* which was the inspiration for John Williams' iconic Star Wars soundtrack.

Holst was one of a number of early 20th century British composers who drew on folk and other influences to write modern, yet accessible new music. Holst would often incorporate the tunes of hymns into his pieces, which isn't surprising as he was choirmaster at a girls' school in England.

This hymn, composed by Holst in 1906, is a beautiful tune inspired by a poem written by Christina Rossetti. The first verse depicts harsh winter weather before going on to tell the Christmas nativity story and is one of the most popular Christmas carols in the United Kingdom.

In my arrangement I keep the accompaniment to a minimum, which allows you to focus on playing the melody. If you are familiar with the carol, think of the words as you play to help with the rhythm and phrasing of the piece.

The bass notes should be allowed to ring out independently of the melody wherever possible. Sustaining bass notes often means keeping one fretting-hand finger held down while the others take care of the melody. The independence to move one finger without the rest jumping up off the fretboard will take time to master.

Bar one makes a great finger independence exercise. Look closely at the rhythms and you'll see the bass note F should continue when the top line rests. Treat each melody note as a separate event to help avoid tension in the fretting hand. Remove the second finger, then place the fourth finger, remove that, then place the first finger.

Example 3a

The fingering directions in bars nine and eleven might seem to make unnecessary use of the weaker fourth finger, but this allows the subsequent notes to be played more smoothly. In any case, the only way to get that unruly fourth finger to play ball is to train it!

Example 3b

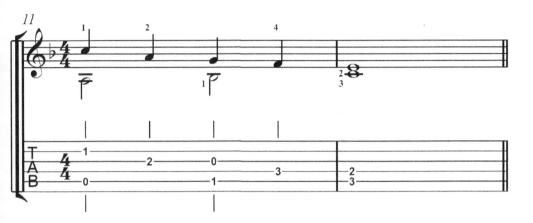

In bar fourteen, play the notes at the 3rd fret with fingers 3 and 4 as indicated. Keeping the hand in the first position makes the transition to the next bar easier and develops good habits.

Example 3c

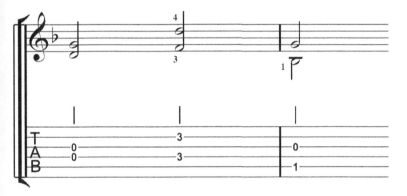

The final F Major chord has a wiggly arrow in front of it. This indicates the notes should be played in succession, rather than simultaneously. Playing the notes of a chord one at time is known as an arpeggio, but this subtle form of embellishment is also called *raking* the chord.

Example 3d

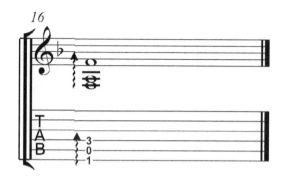

Rest the picking hand thumb on the low E string and push it through the string to rest momentarily on the A string, before falling through that, and repeating the process on the D string.

The first finger of the fretting hand will need to be arched to avoid muting the open A string underneath, so keep the thumb positioned low on the neck.

In the Bleak Midwinter – Gustav Holst

4. Waltz in C Major, Op. 27 – Ferdinando Carulli

Along with Sor, Carulli is one of the most important composers for the classical guitar. He was an experienced teacher and many of his published works are method books and sets of études. The short piece I've selected for this book is from his *Méthode Complète*, (catalogued later as Opus 27).

Carulli was born in Naples, but as an adult lived in Milan and became well known as a performer from a young age and toured Europe widely. He started composing in his early thirties after settling in Paris, which was a world centre of music and culture.

Carulli's "Complete Method" is as comprehensive as it sounds and has been a cornerstone of classical guitar teaching since its publication in 1810. It examines both fretting-hand and picking-hand technique, scales and picking patterns in exhaustive detail, but also intersperses these exercises with charming pieces of music such as this waltz.

This piece introduces several ideas that will be explored later in the book, so it's worth practicing thoroughly.

A waltz is a dance, popular in 18th century Europe, that has a specific rhythm to accompany the steps of the dancers. The melody is organised into bars (measures) containing three beats, rather than the more common four.

If you know your open chord shapes, you'll recognise them here. Although we are only playing one or two notes at a time for much of the piece, the full chord shapes are spelled out gradually.

The example below shows the introduction to the waltz. In bar three, you might recognise the open C Major chord. I've added a couple of notes in brackets to help you see it more clearly, but they're not played in the piece. I've done the same for G7 in the final bar.

Example 4a

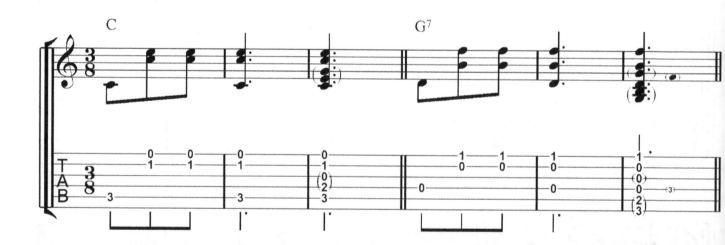

The piece has three, eight-bar sections, each of which have repeat marks (the double line and dots) indicating that they should be played twice before moving on. Break each section down into bitesize pieces that you can repeat and perfect before building up to each eight-bar section.

Once the individual sections of music start to come together, you'll need to know how to order them. The notation includes some musical signposts which direct your way through the piece. These are the repeat bar lines and the *D.C. al fine,* and *Fine* markings.

Obey each repeat mark on the first time through the piece. When you get to the end of the piece, the *D.C. al Fine* sign means return to bar one. D.C. stands for *da capo* in Italian which means "to the head". Continue through the piece, but this time stop at the *Fine* instruction at bar sixteen.

The fretting-hand fingering is generally straightforward. The first finger should play any notes on the 1st fret, the second finger on the 2nd fret, etc. However, there's an instance where the fourth finger should be used on the 3rd fret, because it sets up the bar that follows much more smoothly. The first occurrence of this is in bar four.

The best finger to use is written on the notation near to the note head and, in some of the later pieces, a specific order of fingers is needed to make the music flow smoothly.

Example 4b

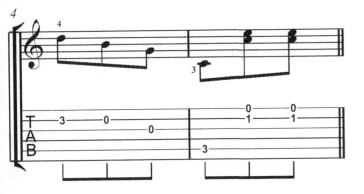

Plucking-wise, most of the piece can be tackled with the thumb, index and middle fingers alone, except in bars 17-18 where there are three consecutive notes on the high string. Here the thumb is used on the open A string, so we enlist the ring finger to help. If this is new ground, try the following short exercise that uses a repeating picking pattern over gradually changing chords. Repeat each bar as many times as you like before moving on to the next.

Example 4c

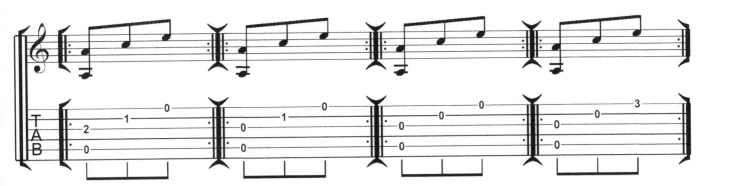

Waltz in C Major, Op. 27 – Carulli

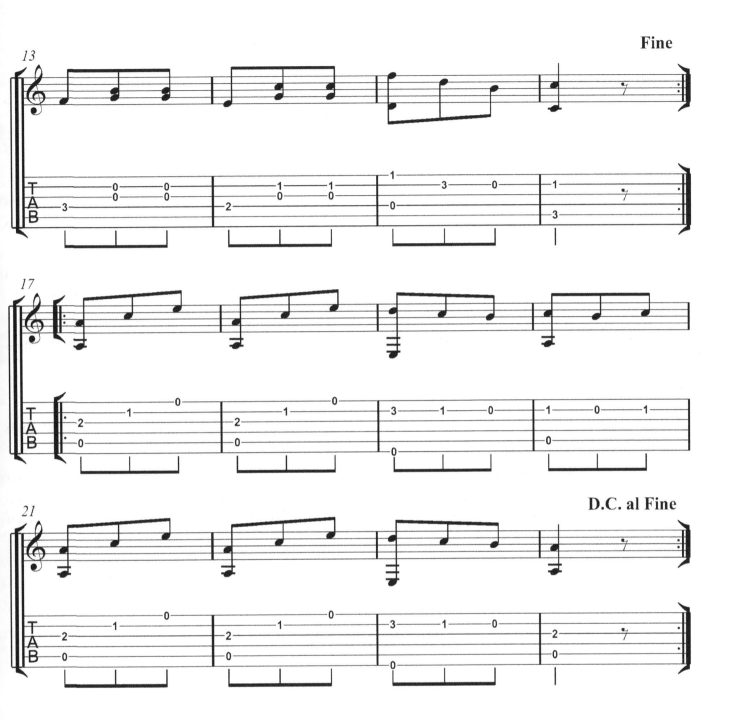

5. Greensleeves – Traditional

Here's one of the most famous traditional English folk tunes. Originally attributed to King Henry VIII of England, it's now thought to date from the slightly later Elizabethan period (1558-1603). Nevertheless, it's quintessentially English and an essential tune in the folk music canon.

The rhythm of the tune is based on a dance, so having confident control of this rhythm is central to giving a good performance.

Most music we encounter has the time signature 4/4, which has four strong crotchet beats in each bar. Each crotchet (1/4 note) can be subdivided into two quavers (1/8ths) or four semiquavers (1/16ths). Time signatures such as 4/4, 3/4 and 2/4 are collectively known as *simple* time signatures.

By contrast, the time signature of Greensleeves is 6/8, which means there are six quaver (1/8th note) beats in each bar. A bar with the time signature 6/8 is split into two strong beats, each subdivided into groups of three. A bar in 6/8 is counted *1 & a 2 & a* (which is easier than counting to six).

Time signatures that are divided into three are called *compound* time signatures. Of these, 6/8 is the most common but others are 3/8, 9/8 and 12/8.

Compound time signatures have a bouncy feel that's perfect for dances.

Once the rhythm is internalised, the notes shouldn't pose too much of a problem as long as you go through carefully and observe the fingering.

The opening phrase of Greensleeves is worth studying before moving on to the rest of the song. The second pair of notes often cause problems to begin with, due to the use of the fourth finger, but do persevere! This sequence is common in a variety of guitar music, so learning to handle it now will make future pieces much easier.

Example 5a

Although we only ever need to play two simultaneous notes in this piece, it's helpful to identify the underlying chords. In bar eleven, this is an open C major chord. Look out for the fingering here. Using the fourth finger means much less shifting around to reach the rest of the melody. Fretting the whole chord will make using the fourth finger feel more natural.

The same approach is used in bar twelve, but moved across onto the B string and low E string (forming a G major chord).

In the following extract I have added the full chords in brackets to help you, but these notes don't sound.

Example 5b

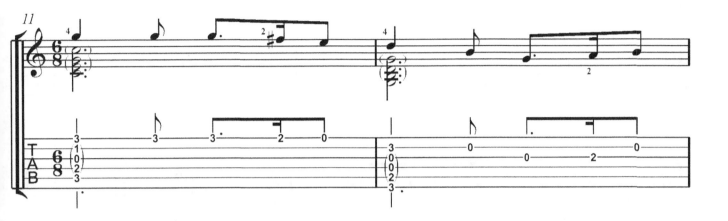

The picking hand should use a combination of thumb and fingers, and make sure to keep the picking hand relaxed over the strings with gently curved fingers, as if you have a tennis ball in your hand. The thumb should play the bass notes shown with downward facing note tails, while the melody is played by the index and middle fingers as necessary.

Greensleeves - Traditional

6. Minuet in G Major – attr. J.S. Bach

The minuet was a popular 3/4 time dance style in the Baroque period and composers would often write concert pieces based on these rhythms.

This famous tune has a complicated history. Though historically attributed to Johann Sebastian Bach, there is a theory that it was composed by the renowned organist Christian Petzold, an acquaintance of the Bach family. The music appeared in a notebook belonging to Bach's wife, Anna Magdalena, containing pieces she had collected. Some of the material in Anna's notebook is attributed to some of the sons of the family, and it was natural to assume that any unmarked material would have been composed by J.S. Bach himself. However, in the 1970s it was confirmed that this tune originated from a harpsichord suite written by Christian Petzold.

Regardless, the tune gives us a wonderful sense of connection with the past when we think that Anna must have heard it three hundred years ago, perhaps at a concert and, having returned home, wrote it down in detail in her notebook.

This music is based on a dance, so once the fingering of the notes has taken shape, focus on keeping an even sense of pulse and rhythm. While minuets might be unfamiliar, the rhythmic feel is not dissimilar to the more common form of the waltz.

Beginners often have difficulty switching smoothly between different rhythmic values. Count "1 & 2 & 3 &…" along to the audio while tapping your foot on the numbers. This can be quite a coordination exercise in itself.

The first two bars provide a good exercise in moving confidently between quavers (1/8th notes) and crotchets (1/4 notes), which repeat in different ways throughout the piece. The second bar's notes should be exactly half the speed of the first bar.

Example 6a

The fingering in bar one might seem awkward at first, but starting with the third and fourth fingers will keep the phrase smooth and connected. Begin by holding a D major chord to find the best hand position for the bar (although when playing you'll just hold down one note at a time).

These classical guitar pieces are often composed of single notes taken from familiar chord shapes and it can help if you can recognise them. The following example breaks down bars 3-7.

Example 6b

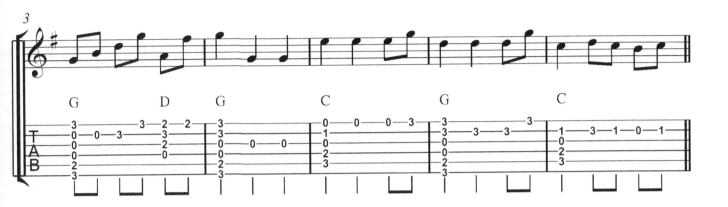

Look out for other chord shapes in the rest of the piece. The B section (starting at bar seventeen) is based around E minor and B7 chords.

I've included fingering directions for other tricky moments, such as bar twenty-three, where three notes on one string occur in quick succession. Spanning all three might feel like quite a stretch, so practise that in short bursts.

The curved line linking together two or more different notes indicates they should be played *legato*, meaning smoothly. In this case using a "hammer-on".

Hammer-ons are performed by bringing a fretting hand finger down onto the string quickly and sounding the note without plucking. The following example is a useful exercise you can play regularly for short periods to develop your finger strength.

Mix up different finger combinations to increase finger dexterity and independence.

Example 6c

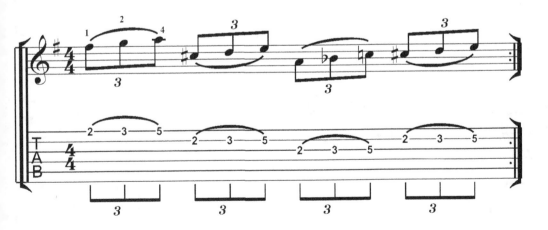

The piece is mainly composed of single notes, but where multiple notes are required, be sure to use the tips of the fingers, to help them to arch naturally and avoid accidentally muting the other strings.

Minuet in G Major – Christian Petzold/J.S. Bach

7. The Four Seasons – Antonio Vivaldi

Antonio Vivaldi (1678-1741) was born in Venice and became one of the most influential Baroque composers of all time. His influence can be heard in the works of J.S. Bach, Mozart, and many others.

The Four Seasons is his best loved work and is a cornerstone of popular classical music. It's actually four separate suites brought together by a programmatic theme. Each season is a separate concerto composed of four movements for solo violin, accompanied by harpsichord and string orchestra.

The pieces are all long, technically demanding, and obviously not written for guitar. However, the tunes contained within them are so memorable and well-loved that I decided to select two of the more famous moments and arrange them for solo guitar.

Even if you think you have never heard of *Spring, 1st Movement* or *Autumn, 1st Movement* from *The Four Seasons*, you'll most likely recognize these two tunes from their many appearances in popular culture. (While I was playing through this arrangement, my partner interrupted me to ask why I was playing "the music from that chocolate advert"!)

Let's start by looking at the form of the piece, as understanding the structure can help us to internalise a piece.

The simplest form is "binary form". As the name suggests, this means that the music alternates between two contrasting musical ideas. We call these the A section and B section. The following figure shows how my arrangement follows binary form during *Spring* movement 1.

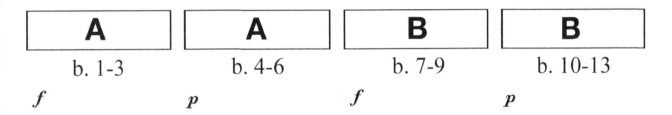

The *Autumn* section follows a different, more subtle structure called "variation form". Here, everything in the piece derives from the first three bars (b. 14-16). Under each variation I have noted what has been done to the initial theme to provide the variation.

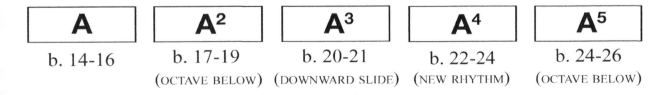

Let's now move on to the notes themselves. The challenge here is that the melody is doubled in thirds, so that each melody note has a harmony note played three notes below. The result is a two-fingered shape which moves along the length of the fretboard.

The way to get comfortable with this movement is to keep the first finger in contact with the high E string throughout, while switching between fingers two and three for the notes on the B string.

Practise playing just the notes on the E string with the first finger to get used to the movement, then add the lower note when you're more confident. The following exercise will teach you to perform this movement.

The first bar contains all the E string melody notes in *Spring*, and the second bar adds the harmony. Keep your hand square to the fretboard as you slide up and down, and try to make the smallest possible movement when swapping between the second and third fingers.

The position shifts should be smooth and relaxed, so don't rush to play the piece too fast. I performed the piece at a more sedate tempo than you might expect of Vivaldi's original work.

Example 7a

Each section of the piece is repeated, but pay attention to the dynamic markings. The bold italic letters indicate whether to play loudly (*f* - *forte*) or softly (*p* - *piano*). This change in dynamics prevents the tune from becoming overfamiliar and the changes in volume and add give a characterful "question and answer" effect to each section.

Example 7b

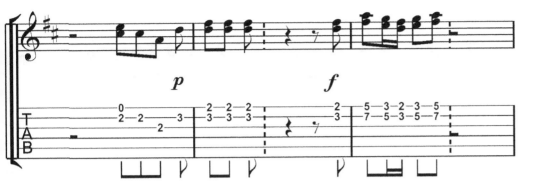

Bars 21-22 contain the biggest position shifts. In bar twenty-one keep the third finger on the B string and slide down the string to the 3rd fret. Bar twenty-two is more of a leap of faith, but with practice you'll become confident with this shift.

Your accuracy will improve if you look at the destination fret before you move, rather than watching your fretting hand. Look out for the suggested fingerings for the final three notes, as these will help you deliver a smooth finale.

The Four Seasons (two extracts) – Antonio Vivaldi

Spring: Movement 1

Autumn: Movement 1

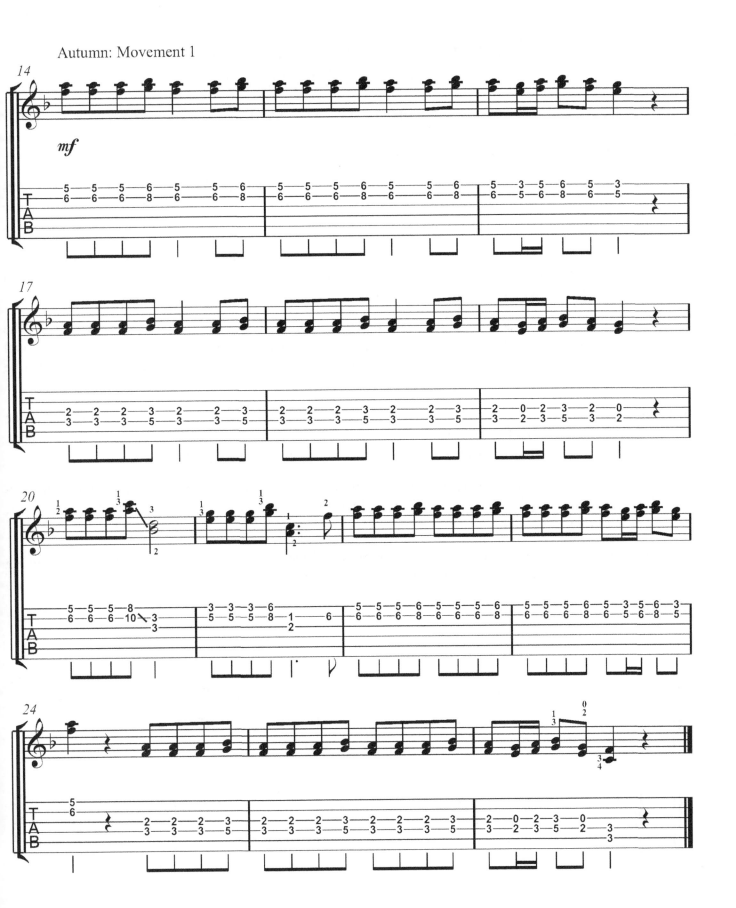

8. Symphony No.9, Mvt. 4 "Ode to Joy" – Ludwig Van Beethoven

Our next piece is the rousing tune from the end of Beethoven's final 1824 symphony No.9, partly inspired by a poem by Friedrich Schiller written in 1785. Beethoven redefined what the symphony could be, and No.9 was ground-breaking in that it included a choir and solo voices.

The tune has since been extracted from its symphonic context and performed internationally at events celebrating freedom, such as the fall of the Berlin wall and the centenary of the end of World War I. It's also the anthem of the European Union.

As such, this piece should be played with a buoyant sense of optimism and energy throughout. Looking at the score you'll see there are some new dynamic directions. The *m* stands for *mezzo* which, when combined with *forte* or *piano*, means "quite loudly" or "quite softly".

The first half of the piece is quite loud, but bars 11-12 should be the loudest moment in the music. The "hairpin" symbol under bar eleven marks a *crescendo*, which means a gradual increase in volume. The final four bars drop to *mp* and should be quieter than the start, but still retain some of the rhythmic energy and drive with which we began.

Performing smooth crescendos and decrescendos (gradually getting quieter) requires extra control in the picking hand, and are created by picking heavily or lightly. There is the tendency to speed up as you get louder, but this should be resisted, so that volume and speed can be controlled independently.

The two exercises below will improve your dynamic range and control. In the first half, play as heavily (loudly) then as lightly (quietly) as you can. This will help define your maximum and minimum volume limits, known as your *dynamic range*.

The double *ff* and *pp* are more extreme versions of our usual *forte* and *piano*. Increasing numbers of *f*'s or *p*'s is uncommon and indicates *exceptionally* loud or quiet moments.

Example 8a

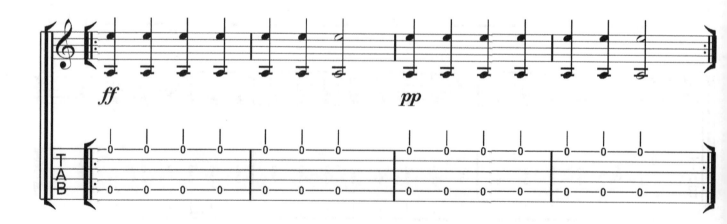

Next, begin as lightly as you can and gradually dig in until you reach the loudest volume you can manage. It's crucial to keep the speed of your plucks as even as possible. As your technique develops, the "gears" you have available will become more and more subtle.

Example 8b

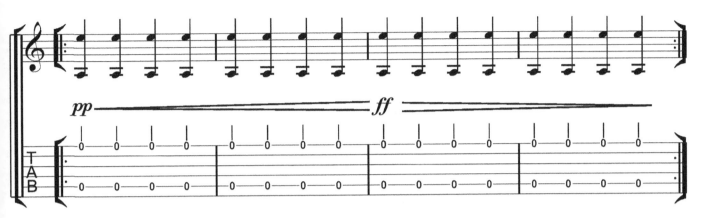

In Ode to Joy, the thumb should pluck all the low notes while the fingers take care of the melody. Focus on synching up the thumb and fingers at the start of each bar with a pinching motion. Where two melody strings are played simultaneously, the first and second fingers (*I* and *M*) should play together.

Conveniently, most of the bass notes use the open D and A strings, so the fretting hand can focus on the melody. However, things get a little trickier towards the end, and bars 11-12 require some careful fingering.

The first chord in bar twelve is discussed both in Sor's Study No. 1 and in Greensleeves. Using fingers two and four here allows what follows to flow more easily.

Another potential trouble spot in bars 13-14 is holding the high A note (5th fret, high E string) with the fourth finger while the bass notes change below it.

In the snippet below, I've included the held notes in brackets so the sequence can be easily seen, and the ties show how long each finger should be held down for. Treat each beat as a separate chord shape and go through the phrases slowly, one motion at a time.

Example 8c

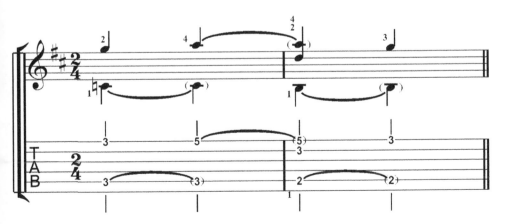

In the final bars there's a dashed line with the word *rit* over the notation. "Rit" is short for *ritardando,* which means a gradual slowing of the tempo. It signals to the listener that the piece is ending and prevents the final chord seeming abrupt. We're so used to hearing pieces end by slowing down that you might do it automatically, but it's important to execute this in a controlled manner.

"Ode to Joy" from Symphony No.9 - Ludwig Van Beethoven

9. Ride of the Valkyries – Richard Wagner

Some musical moments are so dramatic and memorable that they take on a life beyond their original context, and this rousing tune is part of a larger work.

Ride of the Valkyries is from the opera *Die Walküre*. It's a grand orchestral and theatrical work that forms part of Wagner's gargantuan four-opera cycle *Der Ring des Nibelungen* (known as The Ring Cycle). This epic tale features characters from northern European folk mythology, including the Valkyrie, who are powerful female spirits who claim the dead from fields of battle and carry them to Valhalla, the afterlife of Norse warriors.

The rising melodic patterns and galloping rhythms conjure up the approach of the horse-riding Valkyries. These get higher and louder as the piece progresses, and with each ascending motif the Valkyries move closer, assuming epic proportions. Listen to the original orchestral version to hear how characters can be realised in music. Francis Ford Coppola's *Apocalypse Now* (1979) introduced the tune to a new audience, giving it a new association with helicopters and modern warfare.

Like *Greensleeves*, this piece is written in a compound time signature, meaning each beat is broken into three quavers. However, Ride of the Valkyries uses the less common meter of 9/8 which has three beats in each bar that are subdivided into three quavers each. The quavers go by quickly, so count the three strong beats and just feel the subdivisions by getting familiar with the piece.

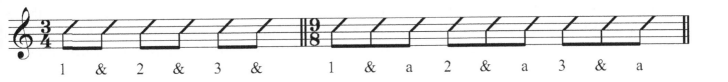

Our solo guitar arrangement sets the scene with minimal accompaniment that suggests the underlying rhythm and the tonic chord of A minor.

The classic rising melody first appears in bar five. The rhythmic groups on beat 1 of each bar looks difficult to count, so listen carefully to my audio and copy it. The second note should feel like a springboard from which we can bounce to get to the high note on beat 2. This rhythm should be plucked with a pinch between *P* and *I*, then a quick *P*, *I*, and *M* for the high note. Occasionally this isn't possible, as in bar seven, so in this case strum the chord with the thumb.

Example 9a

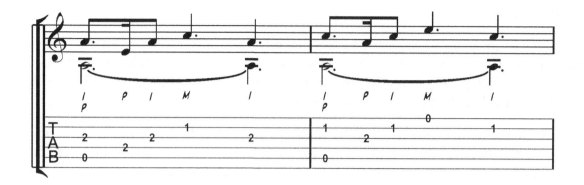

Most of the piece is based around the common open chord shapes: Am, C, G, E and F. To help you identify these I've added chord symbols over the notation. See if you can strum the chords over the audio track to hear how they fit together and make sure you can change fluently between them.

This piece would work brilliantly played as a duet. Get a friend to strum the chords while you pick out the tune from the tab over the top.

The first challenge for the fretting hand is in bar fourteen where we quickly shift position from the 7th fret back to first position. Follow the fingering carefully and it will start to fall into place. The D# note at the 6th fret functions as a halfway point between the two positions and gives the first finger time to change string.

Example 9b

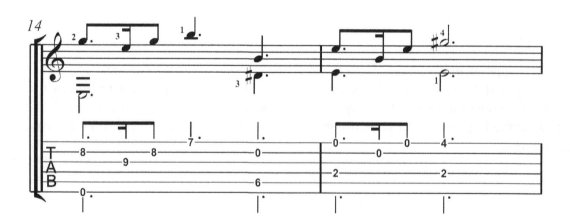

The piece continues with friendly open chords until bar thirty-two, where a barre is needed. Start bar thirty-two with the second and third fingers, so that the first finger is ready and waiting to barre the Am at the 5th fret. Play the first three notes with the tips of the fingers while the Am flattens the first finger against all three strings.

We save the biggest hurdle until last. The scarily named E7b5 chord in bar thirty-four is quite the finger-twister and will take several practice sessions to execute fluently. (Arguably, Wagner's biggest musical innovation was his daring use of dissonant chords and harmonies, which this particularly tense sounding chord hints at).

The fingerings for the preceding Dm chord help us to transition smoothly into it by sliding the first finger down the B-string from the 6th to 5th fret.

When learning new chord shapes, learn to place the fingers in the same order every time to train your muscle memory. The example below shows the best sequence of fingers to play E7b5.

Example 9c

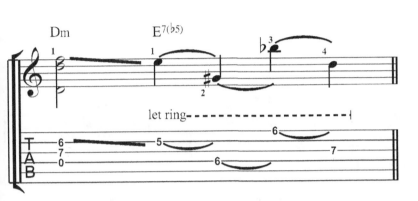

Ride of the Valkyries - Richard Wagner

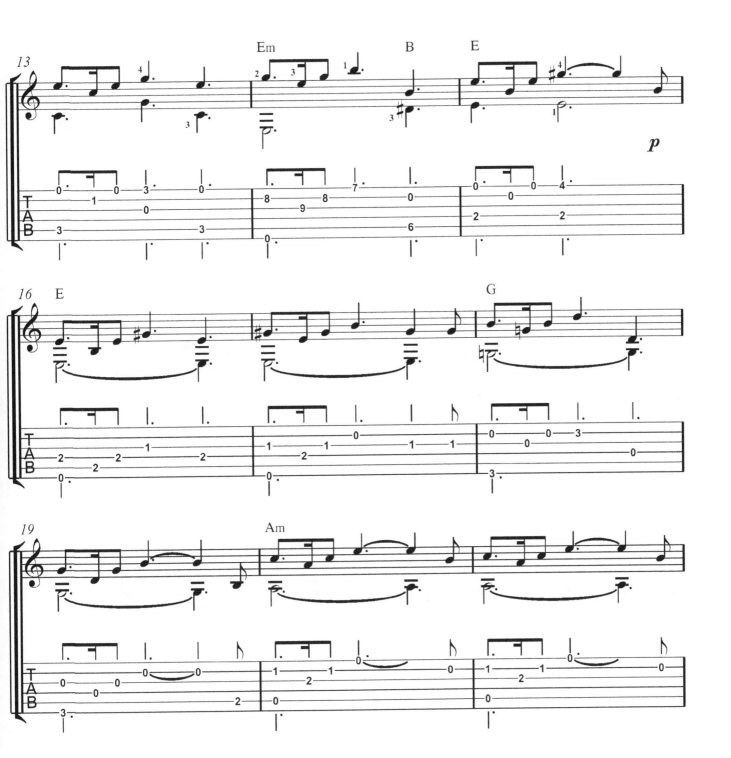

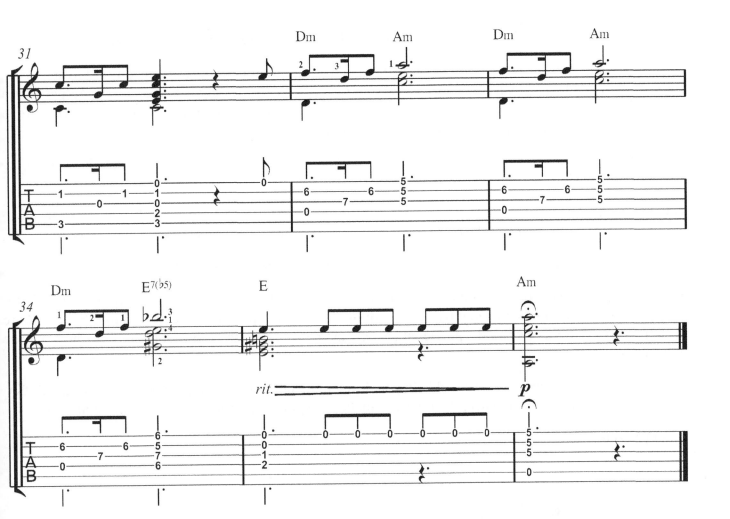

10. In the Hall of the Mountain King – Edvard Grieg

Now to the mountains of Norway for an eerie, foreboding tune from their greatest composer, Edvard Grieg. During the Romantic era, many composers used folk music or stories of their native country in response to a growing sense of national identity, and this is the case with Grieg's most famous piece. This was written for a play called *Peer Gynt* and was based on a native fairy tale.

In the Hall of the Mountain King depicts a point in the story where the protagonist finds himself in the underground kingdom, surrounded by jeering, threatening trolls.

The music superbly captures the sinister footsteps of the trolls. At first, it's light and slow as the trolls move stealthily in the shadows, but as the piece progresses they close in and it gradually becomes louder and faster.

This piece contains new challenges for both hands, especially to achieve the fast tempo.

You'll need to practise slowly to train the fretting hand fingers and maintain the "one-finger-per-fret" rule for the first four bars. Continue this into bars 5-8, with the index finger positioned at the 2nd fret. Bars 9-12 are the biggest challenge as we call the pinkie into action and require a stretch from 1st to 4th fret which may be tough at first.

This fretting hand warmup exercise will help you develop the independence to play with one-finger-per-fret. Start high up on the fretboard where the frets are smaller and gradually work towards the first four frets.

Example 10a

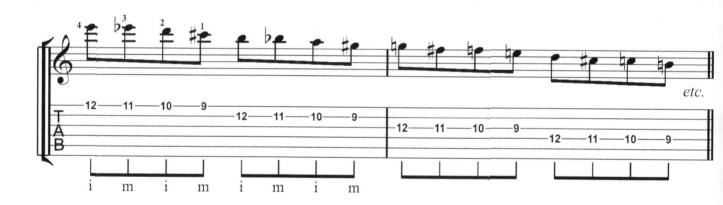

The picking hand has two options. The first is to play each note with the thumb, which will probably be more manageable when learning the tune and will create a softer sound. The second approach is to pluck with *I* and *M*, which is more difficult initially but will help you to achieve more speed. Break each phrase down into small blocks to practise in isolation, such as groups of four notes, then gradually join them together.

The final four bars contain rapid hammer-ons that should be played with the first and second fingers. Keep the first finger held down at the 4th fret and almost immediately bring the second finger down forcefully. This first note is a grace note or *appoggiatura* which is played just before the second and doesn't have its own time value.

Here's an exercise to develop the hammer-on technique needed from bar twenty-three onwards. First play a slow hammer-on so the two notes fall on beats two and three, then speed up to quavers (1/8ths) on "2 &".

Finally, move onto the rapid grace-note.

Example 10b

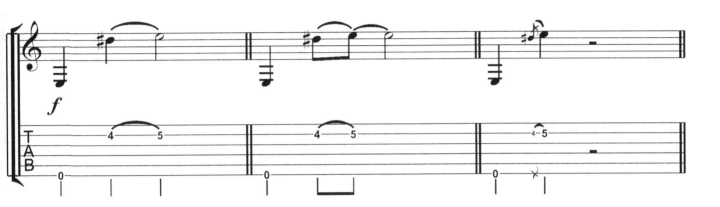

At the end of the piece you should be playing as loudly as possible (*f*). The music burns itself out as the army of trolls close in on Peer Gynt with a series of repeated grace notes in bar 27-28, and a full bar pause in bar twenty-nine before their final attack.

In the original piece for orchestra, this "cliff edge" moment has a drum roll on the timpani and could be copied by using the picking hand fingertips to drum on the body of the guitar.

This piece comes alive with expressive variations in dynamics and tempo, but be sure to only push the speed if you can keep it even and controlled, otherwise it will just sound messy.

In the Hall of the Mountain King - Edvard Grieg

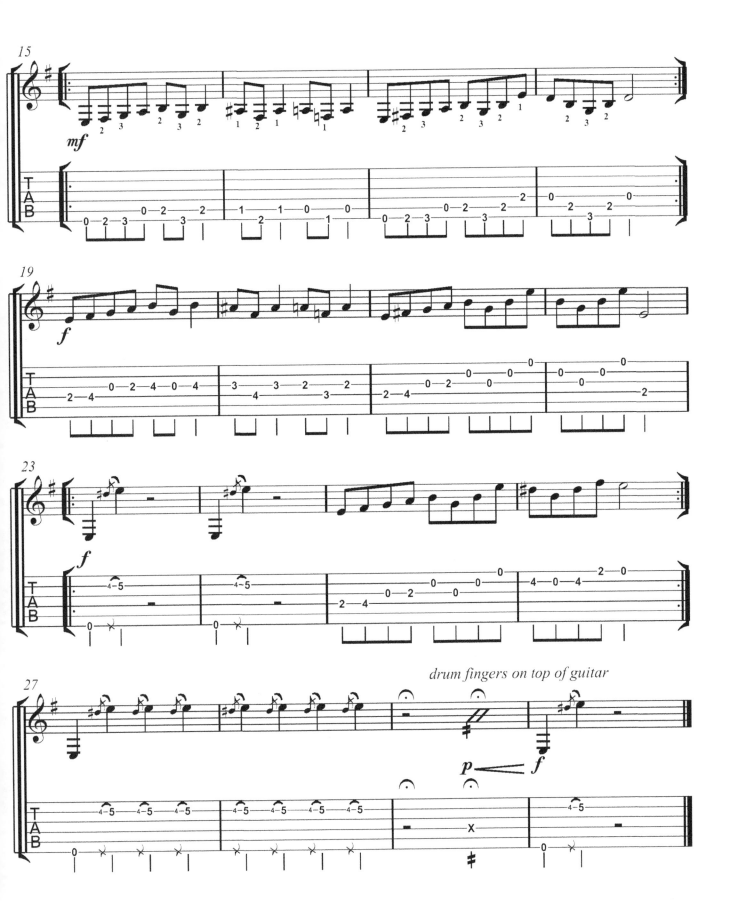

drum fingers on top of guitar

11. Symphony No.40 – W.A. Mozart

Mozart is perhaps the most famous of all classical composers and was famed for being a child prodigy on both the harpsichord and violin. He grew into a mature composer whose body of work is impressively large, especially considering that he died at the age of thirty-five. His compositions include choral pieces, operas, string quartets, keyboard music and, of course, at least forty-one orchestral symphonies, not counting the several that were discovered after his death!

Mozart kept a journal, so we know that Symphony No.40 was finished on 25th July, 1788. The music is uncommon for that period because it's in a minor key. Minor keys sound darker or "sadder" than major keys, and only became more popular during the Romantic movement in the following century.

The version I've arranged for this book focuses on the first theme of the 40th symphony. It moves at a brisk tempo and contains several different sections that will need to be practised separately before linking them together.

The descending two-note phrase that opens the piece is played with a pull-off. This technique allows us to play multiple notes on one string without plucking them and gives the second note a smoother sound.

Example 11a

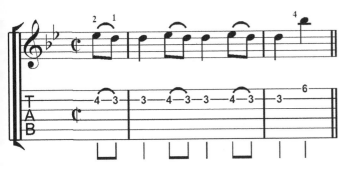

To perform a pull-off, place both the first and second fingers on the fretboard ready at the 3rd and 4th frets of the B string respectively. Pluck the first note before pulling the second downward with flicking motion across the fretboard that will sound the note below. More pull-offs appear in bars five and six using the third and first finger.

There's a tricky but important position shift in bar seven. The previous phrase ends on the 5th fret with the second finger, but the next phrase is best tackled by playing the same note with the fourth finger. During the rest beat, shift the hand down the neck to the 2nd position.

Example 11b

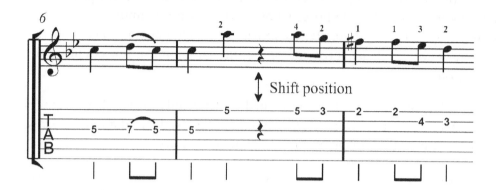

The melody jumps around, so be sure to closely follow the fingering suggestions. For example, in bar eight, swap from the second to the first finger when playing the 3rd fret of the B string. This position shift allows you to reach the next three notes more easily.

The chords in bars 19-20 change quickly, so slide the second finger back and forth on the B string, adding the first finger then third finger in a similar fashion to the earlier *Four Seasons* arrangement.

Example 11c

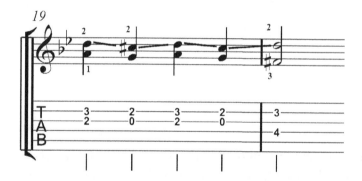

The most challenging moment in the piece occurs in bar thirty-four, which repeats three times. The ascending melody will take time to develop, so be patient. All four fretting hand fingers are needed, so keep a "square-on" hand position, so that each finger is positioned over its own fret. The picking hand should be alternating first and second fingers.

The exercise below shows how to practise this section in fragments. Repeat each bar at a slow tempo before connecting them. The first finger should slide up the high E string from fret 5 to fret 6, allowing the stretch to the 9th. To reset, land on the second finger at the 6th fret.

Example 11d

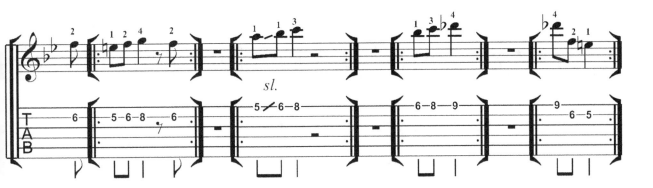

The final descending pattern also challenges the picking hand. Start by alternating two fingers, then switch to the thumb for the notes on the D (fourth) string. Here's an easier alternative ending using a C7 chord shape. Its picking pattern is a steppingstone to your playing my recorded version.

Example 11e

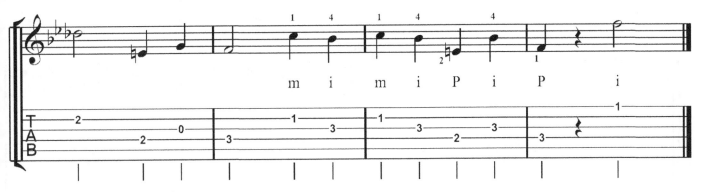

Symphony No.40, Mvt. 1 – W.A. Mozart

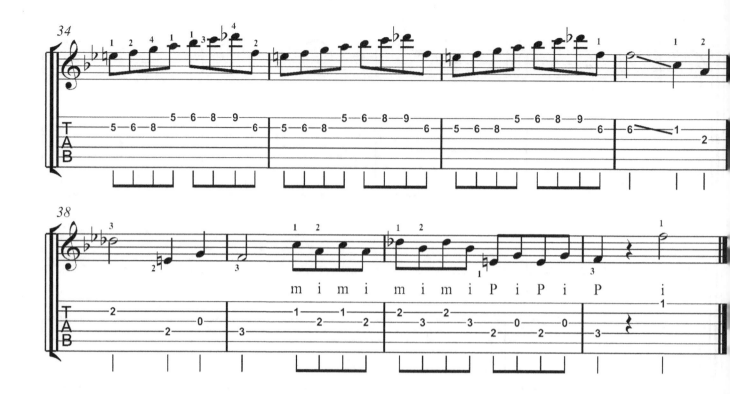

12. Study No.9, Op. 35 – Fernando Sor

This Sor study is an excellent fingerpicking workout and is taken from *24 Easy Studies Op. 35* which was published in 1828.

It uses a repeating four-note picking pattern of *P* (thumb), *I* (index), *M* (middle) and *I* (index), regardless of which strings are played to give a consistent tone.

If picking with several fingers is new, practise the movement slowly on the first chord shape or with open strings. Start with the top three (thinnest) strings and then relocate the thumb to the lower strings.

Example 12a

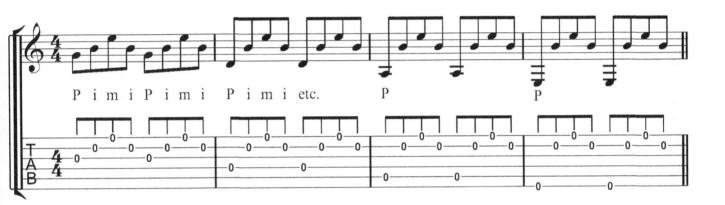

Try combining the above exercise with the crescendo exercise described earlier in Beethoven's *Ode to Joy*.

The fretting hand has several new chord shapes to learn and the first is in bar two. The non-standard fingering for the open A chord (a barre in this instance) should be placed ahead of time, during the D chord in the first half of the bar.

Example 12b

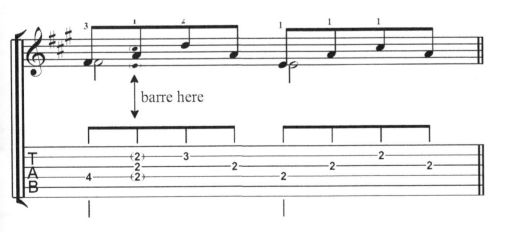

Bar six has two unusual shapes that are shown below as block chords. Follow the fingering directions in the tab to link the chord shapes together smoothly. Your hand position is crucial to making these chords comfortable. Tilting the palm towards yourself will make the first shape easier, while tucking the elbow in and rolling the palm away will allow the pinky to reach the A string in the second chord.

In bar seven there's a full B major barre chord. Barre chords take time to perfect and hand strength plays a key role, particularly on steel string guitars. Pull the guitar body in against your ribs, rather than simply squeezing the neck between fingers and thumb. Using the bigger muscles in the shoulder and bicep takes the strain off your digits, gives more control, and helps reduce the risk of strain injuries.

The following example reduces bars 6-7 to block chords and isolates the fretting hand movements.

Example 12c

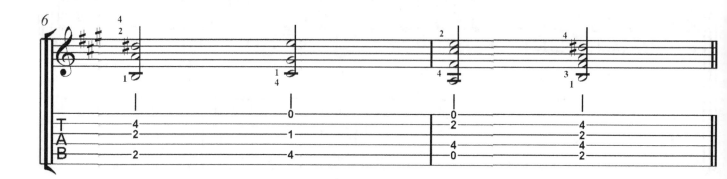

The regular picking pattern is interrupted in bar sixteen. At this point alternating *P, I, P, I, P* is be the best approach.

In the notation you'll spot that the first and fifth quaver (1/8th) notes in each bar are doubled by a longer minim. Solo guitar music often contains several musical parts played simultaneously and these lines are written as individual rhythms, so you know how long each note should last.

The note is only played once, but you should keep it held so it sustains under the next four notes, linking as smoothly as possible to the next bass note.

Example 12d

Longer pieces like this should be broken down into small chunks and mastered slowly. Working on a few isolated sections until they are fluent will make the music much more attainable. As you work through the study, several key phrases will reappear and this repetition creates a sense of form and structure for the listener. Analyse the piece by colour coding or otherwise labelling each occurrence of these phrases.

Study No.9, Op. 35 - Fernando Sor

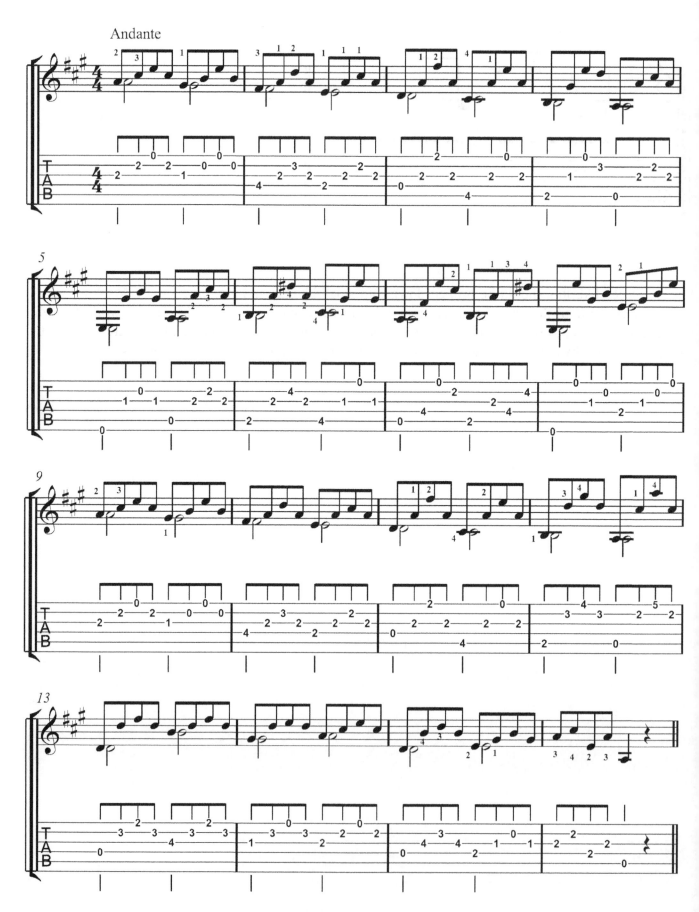

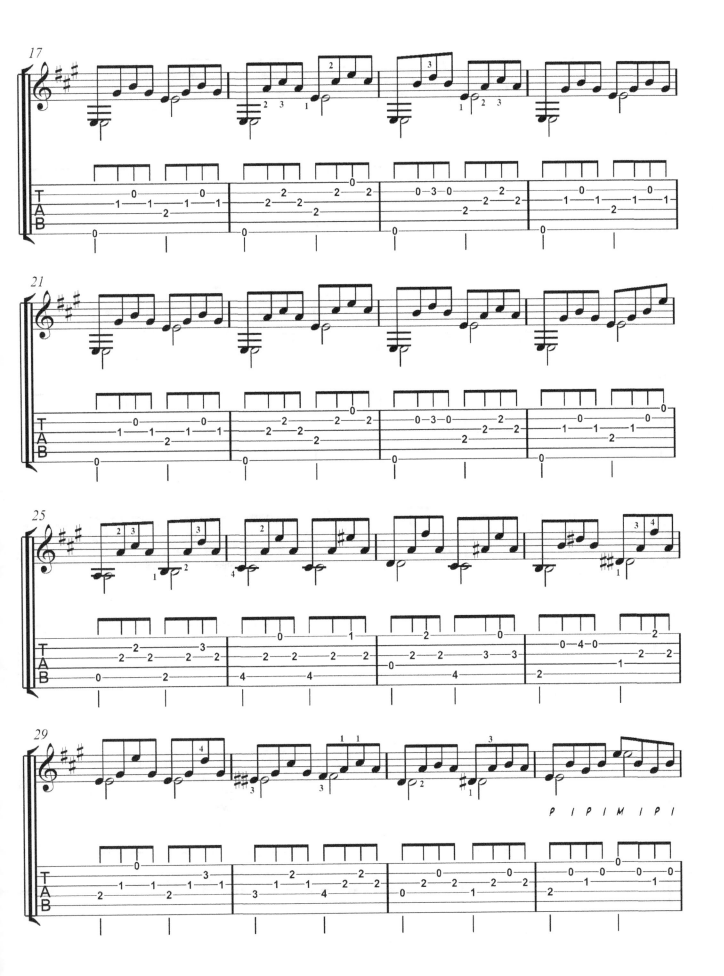

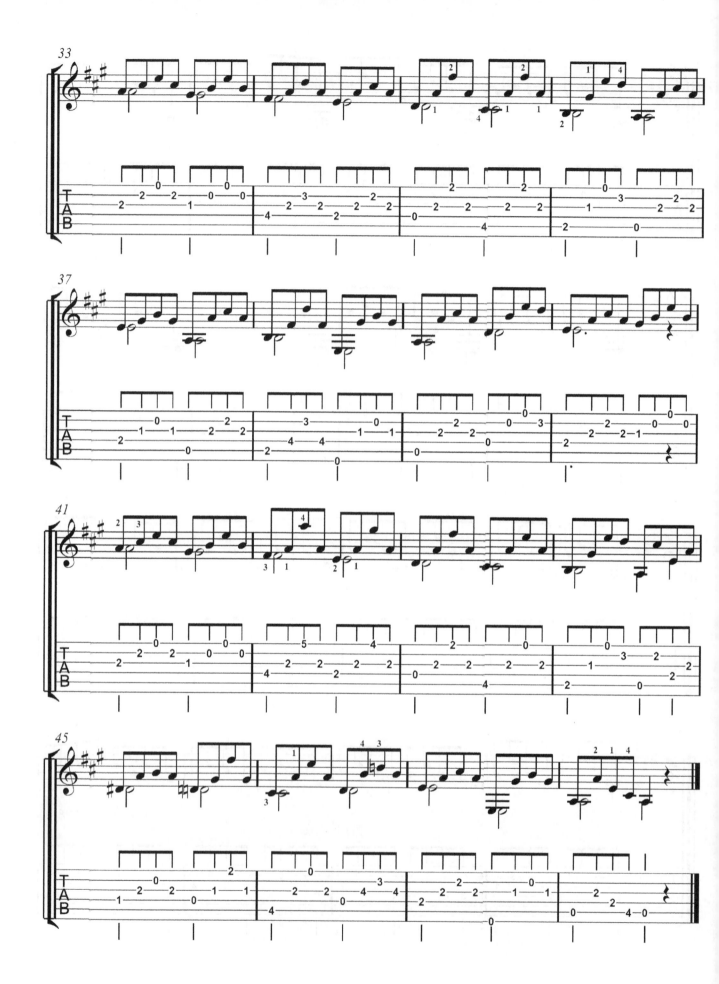

13. Für Elise – Ludwig van Beethoven

Now for one of the most well-known of all these musical pieces: *Für Elise*. This short piano piece was only discovered forty years after Beethoven's death and the identity of Elise is unknown. Indeed, it may have actually been "Therese" on the original score. Beethoven had a pupil called Therese Malfatti with whom he was in love.

Für Elise was published as a bagatelle in 1867, as part of the book *Neue Briefe Beethovens* (New letters by Beethoven) by scholar Ludwig Nohl. A *bagatelle* is a term for any short, playful piece of classical music and doesn't refer to mood or rhythm.

Our bagatelle has a time signature of 3/4 which gives it a flowing dance-like phrasing. My arrangement is based on just the A section of the whole bagatelle, as this is the most memorable and guitar-friendly section of the piece.

Listen to the original and you'll hear the intro phrase return several times, interspersed with different episodes that don't repeat. This form is known as *Rondo*, one of the most common musical forms and a development of the simpler "binary form" we encountered in *The Four Seasons*. Rondo form can be pictured as a main melody (A) rotated with other material labelled B, then C etc.

Although we'll only be playing the A section, this in itself has a mini binary structure of AABA. The first eight bars of the piece are played twice, with a 1st and 2nd time ending. Then, fresh material acts as a bridge before returning to a final repeat of the first eight bars.

Eagle-eyed readers might have spotted that the first bar contains only two quaver (1/8th) notes. This is a pickup or *anacrusis*, and doesn't count towards the numbering of the bars. It can help to count yourself in to such pieces to establish a solid pulse. Happy Birthday (also in 3/4) is another example of an anacrusis. The third note (**birth**-day) is in fact the downbeat of the tune.

Look at bar eight and see how the same pickup notes are included at the end of the bar, which circles back to bar one.

Example 13a

The intro phrase will probably be the most challenging part of this piece so it's worth spending time getting it right. The first example below isolates each of the important details.

The first two notes (E and D#) are a semitone (1 fret) apart. It might seem easier to play them on the same string, but playing them between the E and B strings makes the plucking easier and means no change of fretting hand position.

Secondly, there's a pull-off from the 3rd to 1st fret, so the index finger must be placed on the 1st fret before pulling-off with the ring finger. The pull-off gives the plucking hand a moment to address the third sticking-point:

Look at the plucking directions in the music. The index and thumb alternate to begin with, then need to pinch together on the A and G strings in bar two. This repositioning of the picking hand will take some training to become automatic, but the pull-off will make the transition easier.

Example 13b

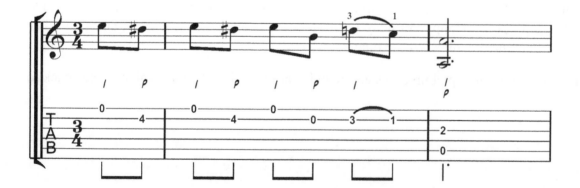

After the famous opening, the music moves back and forth between the chords of Am and E major. In bars two and six the thumb should be used for the notes on the A string and the D string, so the index finger is ready for the G string and the middle finger on the B string in the following bar.

The B section contains a pickup phrase consisting of the three notes at the end of bar nine. It's important to think of these as linking to the following bar's notes, not as a part of the previous section.

There are more wide interval "chords" in this section. Playing them without the additional melody notes gives you a skeleton framework upon which you can later hang the melody. The second bar in this extract might normally be fretted with third and fourth finger, but in this instance the third will be needed on the D string later in the bar.

Example 13c

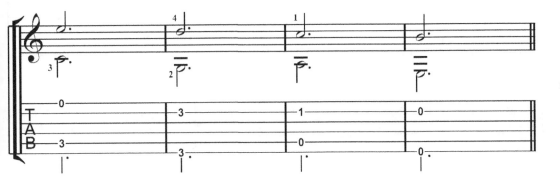

Für Elise – Ludwig van Beethoven

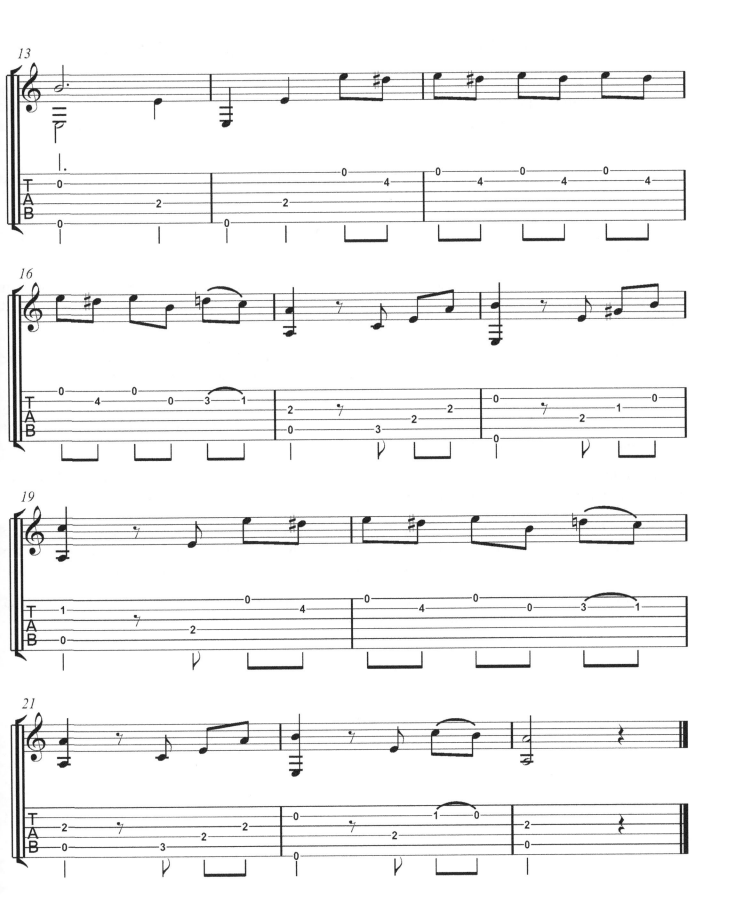

14. Theme from the 24th Caprice – Niccolo Paganini

Italian violinist Niccolo Paganini was one of the most renowned performers of the 19th century. His prodigious ability on the instrument combined with brilliant showmanship earned him a fearsome reputation. He was reputed to have sold his soul to the devil in exchange for his talent, a myth that would later also be applied to pioneering blues guitarist Robert Johnson.

Paganini was also an accomplished guitarist and composed many pieces for both instruments. Many of these pieces are intensely challenging, even for advanced players. Thankfully, this tune is much more accessible! The 24th Caprice is probably his best-known work and English composer Andrew Lloyd Webber famously arranged a rocked-up version for the theme music to *The Southbank Show*, a popular, long-running arts review show on British television.

Paganini's flair and flamboyance turned him into the rock star of his time and since the 1980s there has been a resurgence of interest in his work amongst heavy metal guitarists, with many of his Caprices being arranged for electric guitar. Yngwie Malmsteen incorporated part of Paganini's 4th Violin Concerto into his set list.

If you listen to the audio and examine the score, you'll see there are two main sections: an A section and the contrasting B section. The same one-bar rhythmic motif is used throughout while the melody develops.

Follow the fingering at the end of bar two, repeated in bar six, to get a smooth transition from the D string to G string at the 2nd fret. Using both the first and second finger on the 2nd fret helps to avoid a pause that might occur if the same finger were to jump from one string to the other.

Starting at bar nine, the B section is slightly harder because the fretting hand covers more of the fretboard. Fingerings have been added to help you through these challenging position shifts.

The second phrase in the B section ends on the fourth finger. Quickly swap this for the first finger to reach the following note at the 5th fret. The first finger must then slide down the fretboard to the 1st fret. Hold down the string with enough pressure to keep the note ringing out as you slide without re-plucking the string.

The melody works well when unaccompanied, but I have added appropriate chords over the top of the staff so you can perform this as a duet with another instrument.

Theme from the 24th Caprice - Nicolo Paganini

15. Slavonic Dance No.1 – Antonín Dvořák

Here is another dance-inspired piece, this time from Czech composer Antonín Dvořák. Dvořák (pronounced *dvor-shack*) was born in 1841 in a town near Prague, which was then part of the Austrian Empire. He gained international recognition for his symphonies, string quartets and choral work, and travelled widely to conduct performances. Later in life Dvořák moved to America to teach at the New York Conservatoire, and it was during this time that his most enduring pieces were composed, such as his Symphony No.9 (The *New World* Symphony), and String Quartet No.12 (The *American* Quartet).

The set of Slavonic Dances that we're looking at here was an early success, published in 1878 after winning a competition judged by Austrian composer Brahms, whose famous *Hungarian Dances* were an inspiration. As with other Romantic composers, national identity was important and folk references were common.

Unlike Brahms, who took his Hungarian tunes from a popular collection, Dvořák's pieces quote no traditional material, but manage to encapsulate the distinctly Bohemian (rather than Slavic) style. These days they are most commonly performed as bombastic, sweeping orchestral pieces, but they were originally written for two players sitting at one piano.

Here is the first dance of Op. 46 written in G Major to better suit the guitar's tuning and avoid high notes. I've also shortened some sections, although this is still the longest piece in the book.

Dance No. 1 is a driving rhythmic piece in 3/4 known as a *furiant*. A defining characteristic of the dance is the phrasing, which Dvořák emphasises.

The A section uses a repeating two-bar rhythm that totals six beats. A standard waltz would reinforce a "**1** 2 **3 1** 2 3" count, but the Furiant gets its character from grouping each six-beat phrase into three groups of two, rather than two groups of three.

The B section (bars 10-17) restores a "standard" 3/4 feel.

Listen to the audio to hear how different the feel is from the waltz and minuet. The phrasing and counting is shown more clearly below, although achieving familiarity through listening is the best approach to feeling the music.

Example 15a

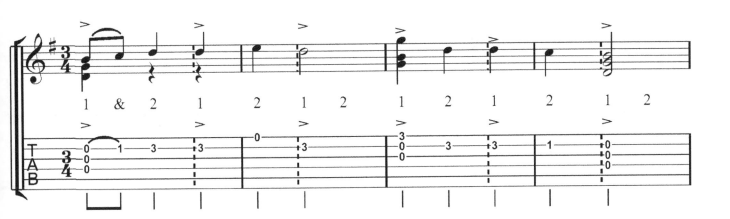

The B section calls for a one-finger-per-fret approach. It takes time to build the stamina to keep the fretting hand stretched at the 1st fret, so try this warm-up exercise to help your development. Use the same fingers in each bar, but move the phrase slowly down the fretboard, which will widen the stretch gradually as you descend. Try to keep the hand open, with each finger hovering over its assigned fret throughout.

Example 15b

Notice how the C section (bars 20-28) borrows the rhythm and overall shape of the initial tune but uses different notes. This is known as *development* or *variation* on a theme.

The following extract is of bars 25-28 which conclude the C section and includes some block chords which can be strummed or fingerpicked. The fingering shows the most efficient way to navigate them. Some of the shapes are quite common and I've labelled them here. Look out for the first finger barre throughout bar twenty-seven. In bar twenty-eight, a D major shape is used at the 7th fret. Slide the 2nd finger on the B string to transition smoothly from this D shape to the second shape in bar twenty-eight.

Once the shapes are well memorised, try to make them a bit more expressive. The first chord in each bar has a small dot over it, meaning it should be cut short by releasing the finger pressure quickly after being plucked. This is known as playing *staccato*. The combination of short/long notes provides a sense of bounce that moves the piece forward.

Example 15c

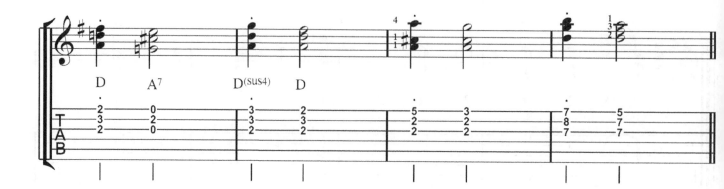

A simpler chord section occurs in bars 44-47. This phrase repeats an A minor to E minor chord change. Keep the 2nd finger common to both chord shapes on the D string to help anchor your fretting hand.

The final variation on the tune starts at bar forty-eight and contrasts with the rest of the piece by placing the melody in the bass with accompanying notes on the higher strings. This will challenge your thumb, so leave out the higher open strings to begin with and just practise playing the notes with downward facing stems with your thumb.

Example 15d

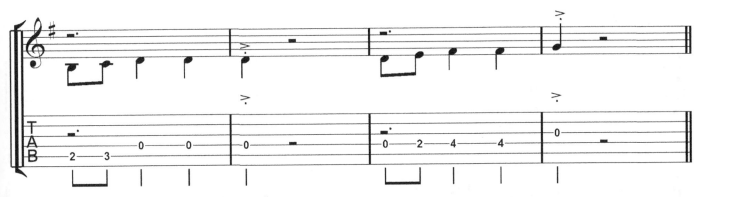

Slavonic Dance Op. 46, No.1 – Anton Dvořák

16. Hornpipe – George Frederick Handel

Water Music was composed in 1717 by George Frederick Handel. It comprises three suites, the first being in F Major. Water Music was first performed for King George I of England on a boat trip along the river Thames in London.

Though Handel is considered one of the most important English classical composers. alongside Purcell and Elgar, he was in fact born in Germany (like King George I). Handel lived in Hamburg and Italy before moving to England, eventually becoming a naturalised British citizen. His style was characteristic of the Baroque period and greatly influenced the next generation of composers, such as Haydn and Mozart.

A hornpipe is now more commonly associated with folk music, but variations date back to the court dances of the 1600s.

The time signature is 3/2, which means that the bar is broken up into three even beats, each lasting for a half note (minim). The Minuet in G in Chapter Six is in 3/4 time and the feel of these two time-signatures is identical, but the 3/2 time signature can be used to cram more notes into each beat and keeps the page cleaner and easier to read.

To illustrate this, the two bars below sound identical, but the 3/2 bar looks less complicated. Compare the top row of notes in each of the two bars and you'll see that the second bar has one horizontal tail removed from every note.

Example 16a

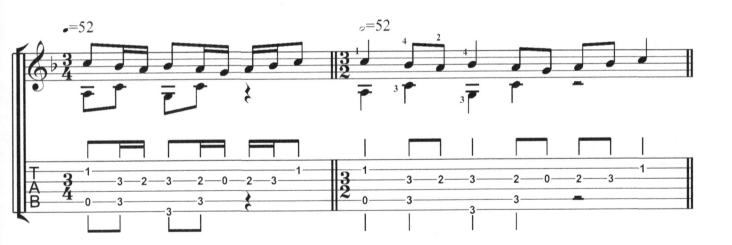

This hornpipe includes wide intervals, so the same practice tips from earlier pieces will help you.

In particular there's a lot of movement between the fourth and first finger on the high strings while holding a lower note with the third. The following exercise for the fretting hand will familiarise you with the combinations needed. Focus on moving just one finger at a time and take it slowly at first.

Example 16b

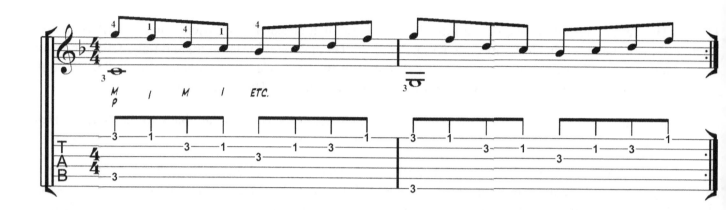

There are several moments where the pinky finger slides along the high E string to change position. It's important to fret the string with the fingertip and arch the fingers throughout.

Familiarise yourself with the two shapes below in isolation and find an angle of the hand that allows you to reach the notes comfortably. The first interval will be played with a horizontal palm. For the second, the palm is likely to be turned to a vertical position, like giving a handshake. Move between the two shapes remembering how the whole hand and wrist need to turn. The fourth finger should act like a fulcrum around which the hand can rotate.

Example 16c

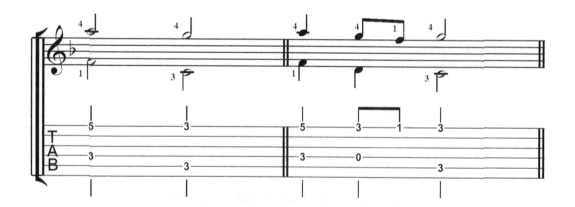

A similar technique is used in bar fifteen, where the second finger slides down the G string while swapping the third finger for the first finger. Breaking these transitions down into one-finger-at-a-time processes will help you get the motion as smooth and efficient as possible.

Finally, there's a descending sequence in bar eleven that includes pull-offs and slides with the first finger. Here, a three-note pattern occurs three times starting on the 6th, 5th and 3rd frets.

Example 16d

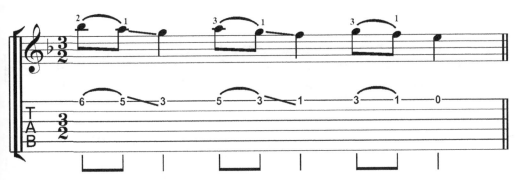

The audio track I've provided is slower than typical orchestral performances. Listen to other versions for inspiration and gradually speed up as you get more familiar with the piece.

Hornpipe from Water Music – G.F. Handel

D.C. al Fine

17. Pictures at an Exhibition (Promenade) – Modest Mussorgsky

Modest Mussorgsky was a Russian composer active in the mid-19th century who lived mostly in Saint Petersburg. Like many of his contemporaries, Mussorgsky aimed to create distinctly "Russian" music using folklore and traditional tunes while avoiding western European traits.

Mussorgsky is less of a household name than some of the big hitters we've looked at so far, but several of his compositions have remained popular and may well be familiar to you. The most famous of these are the suite *Pictures at An Exhibition*, and *Night on Bald Mountain*, which was used in Disney's animated 1940 movie *Fantasia*.

The pieces I've included here are taken from *Pictures at an Exhibition*. Originally a collection of pieces for solo piano depicting a walk through a gallery of paintings by Russian artist Victor Hartmann, this was later arranged for orchestra by French composer Maurice Ravel, and it's this version that is now most often heard. *Promenade* acts as an interlude between each of the ten paintings.

The rock band Emerson, Lake & Palmer arranged the suite with Greg Lake writing lyrics to the most melodic sections including Promenade. Disney's *Fantasia* was re-released in 1969, which likely ignited psychedelic rock musicians' interest in composers like Mussorgsky, Stravinsky and Tchaikovsky.

Changing time signatures and using little direct repetition tends to make music less accessible, yet Promenade is instantly hummable. Thankfully, the time signatures shouldn't be a cause for alarm. The rhythm is regular and with repeated listening to the audio track, the phrasing of the tune will quickly sink in.

As described in *Greensleeves*, time signatures with a top number of 6 are compound meters and divided into groups of three. Much of the piece is in 6/4 with occasional bars in 5/4. The two bars shown below (bars 9 and 11) contain the same rhythm and notes, but the second time around it is cut short by one note, resulting in the 5/4 bar.

Example 17a

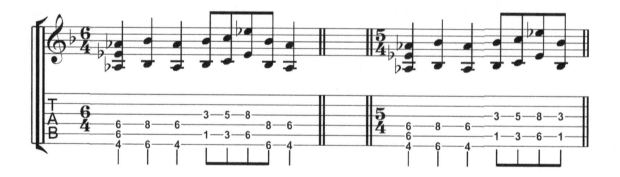

In bar three there is a sudden change in dynamics. After the first two bars' unassuming tune without any accompaniment (marked *p* for piano – to be played gently), the chords on the low strings come crashing in to make a strong contrasting impression. The *sub* instruction is short for *subito*, or "suddenly", and emphasises that there should be no gradual crescendo from quiet to loud.

There are several occasions where one note is held down and the melody moves above it. Breaking these sections down into individual movements will help to teach the fretting hand the movements you can make with one finger occupied. These two exercises do exactly that and are based on bars six and eight of *Promenade* respectively.

The principle is to play the melody without using the finger that will eventually have to hold the bass note. The fingerings show we must avoid finger three in the first bar. The second bar is a development where the low note is included, but not played simultaneously.

The first example reserves the third finger to play the low note. The second example uses the first finger for the low note. Some rotating of the wrist is needed in the fourth bar, as a different hand position is needed for each use of the second finger.

Example 17b

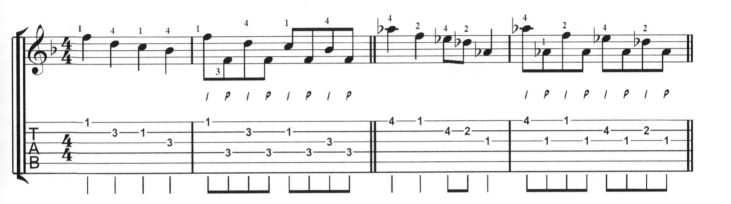

The crux of the piece is bar thirteen. The quick succession of different chord shapes might look intimidating on the page, and it will take practice before you get through it with confidence, but it is very playable if you stick to the written fingerings. In the following exercise, the lines between chords show when the third finger remains on the B string. Concentrate on placing the other fingers around the third finger.

Example 17c

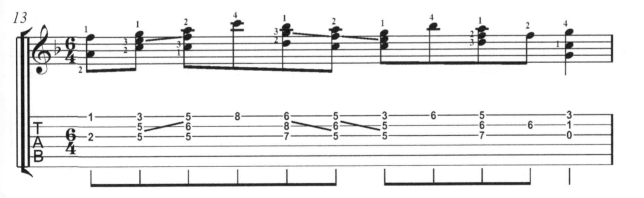

Bar ten provides a slightly easier variation on the same chord change.

Promenade – Modest Mussorgsky

18. Great Gate of Kiev – Modest Mussorgsky

Mussorgsky's *Pictures at an Exhibition* is a ten-part suite and now we'll learn another of the famous tunes from *Pictures...* the tenth and final scene, *Great Gate of Kiev,* also known as *The Bogatyr Gates.*

Great Gate of Kiev refers to a painting by Victor Hartmann. The majestic stone arch was never in fact constructed, but the painting was Hartmann's suggestion for a commemorative arch in the Ukrainian city. Art and music always inspire each other, so think about the stability and grandeur of the image and how this could be conveyed in a musical performance.

To begin with, we'll untangle the musical structure. Look through the piece to locate the two repeat-bar symbols. They both signal a return to the start of the piece. You'll also notice brackets extending over the top of the notation marked 1. 2. and 3. These are alternative endings that should be taken in turn following the return to the start.

After performing bar four for the second time, skip immediately to bar nine (the 2nd time bracket), play through to bar seventeen, then return to bars 1-4 for the third time, this time skipping to the 3rd time ending at bar eighteen. The 3rd time bracket is open ended, which tells us there are no further repeats.

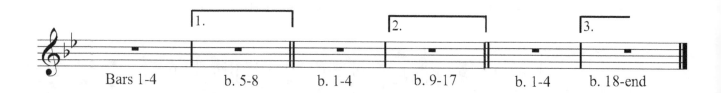

Before diving into the piece, prime your fretting hand for the passages found in bars six, nine and fourteen (and others) by using this exercise.

Example 18a

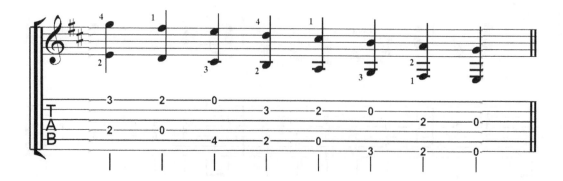

I limited this arrangement to two-note chords that played in a regular rhythm until bar twenty-two, where a series of four-note open chords are used to bring the piece to a climax.

In bar twenty-four we have a regular open D major chord, but in order to flow seamlessly into the following B minor chord it should be played by barring the notes on the 2nd fret with the first finger.

The first finger remains in position at the 2nd fret of the G string from bar twenty-one onwards, but each chord shape might need some hand and arm repositioning to fret them cleanly.

Example 18b

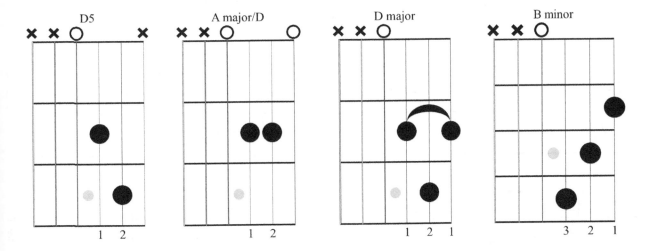

These chord shapes should be played loudly and with confidence to create the high point of the piece. Notice how dynamics provide variation to the repeated phrase in bars 20-21.

After the climactic strummed chords, the piece can be allowed to die away quietly. To help with this expressive aspect the piece uses *harmonics*.

A harmonic is a special kind of note played by lightly touching strings above certain frets. These notes produce clear bell-like chimes and the easiest place to play them are at the 12th and 7th frets.

Use the pad of the finger to touch the string *directly over* the 12th fret (over the fret-wire, rather than between the frets where you would usually play). Pick the string then remove the finger from the string as quickly as possible to allow the harmonic to ring.

Because the finger doesn't remain in contact with the string the harmonics in bars 30-31 can ring together, so long as you are careful not to accidentally mute the B string when reaching for the A string.

Great Gate of Kiev was originally written in the key of Eb, but I've rewritten it in the key of D so it fits more comfortably onto the guitar. If you'd like to perform it in the original key place a capo at the 1st fret and play all the notes in the tab one fret higher than written.

The Great Gate of Kiev – Mussorgsky

Closing Words

I hope you've enjoyed exploring the pieces in this book as part of your journey towards playing classical guitar. Building a repertoire of pieces is rewarding and will give you confidence to tackle new and more challenging music.

There are other aspects of musicianship that will improve your ability and make learning new pieces quicker, easier and more fun. Those skills include…

Physical technique (training the hands to fret and pluck cleanly and quickly).

Music theory (reading notation, locating notes on the fretboard and understanding chord names and symbols).

Ear training (recognising the intervals between different pitches and recalling rhythms).

We've covered a broad range of music from Baroque to Irish folk, along with different playing styles such as chord-based pieces, unaccompanied melodies, and contrapuntal arrangements. I recommend that you persevere with at least one piece in each style before moving on, because each approach has something to teach you. Over time you'll find that some styles appeal to you more than others and this will help you decide on your future focus.

The other two books in my classical guitar repertoire series, *First Pieces for Classical Guitar* and *Intermediate Pieces for Classical Guitar* continue the musical ideas we have examined in this carefully curated set of pieces. They gradually increase the number of simultaneous notes and position shifts you'll experience, and increasingly emphasise your picking hand development. They explore music written more specifically for guitar including composers such as Fernando Sor, Mauro Giuliani and Francisco Tárrega, as well as my arrangements of famous folk tunes.

Please do re-visit the music in this book every now and then, because as you grow as a musician you'll add new dimensions to older pieces, and gain the confidence to make your own variations to my arrangements.

Good luck on your guitar playing journey.

Rob Thorpe.

By the Same Author

First Pieces for Classical Guitar

Intermediate Pieces for Classical Guitar

Guitar Pedals – Mastering Guitar Effects

Heavy Metal Lead Guitar

Heavy Metal Rhythm Guitar

Progressive Metal Guitar

The Heavy Metal Guitar Bible

Made in the USA
Monee, IL
23 May 2022